SCHOLASTIC

READ & RESPOND

Bringing the best books to life in the classroom

Activities based on **Millions**

By Frank Cottrell Boyce

T0322916

Terms and conditions

IMPORTANT – PERMITTED USE AND WARNINGS – READ CAREFULLY BEFORE USING

This CD-ROM has been tested for viruses at all stages of its production. However, we recommend that you run virus-checking software on your computer systems at all times. Scholastic Ltd cannot accept any responsibility for any loss, disruption or damage to your data or your computer system that may occur as a result of using either the CD-ROM or the data held on it.

IF YOU ACCEPT THE ABOVE CONDITIONS YOU MAY PROCEED TO USE THE CD-ROM.

Recommended system requirements:
Windows: XP (Service Pack 3), Vista (Service Pack 2), Windows 7 or Windows 8 with 2.33GHz processor
Mac: OS 10.6 to 10.8 with Intel Core™ Duo processor
1GB RAM (recommended)
1024 x 768 Screen resolution
CD-ROM drive (24x speed recommended)
Adobe Reader (version 9 recommended for Mac users)
Broadband internet connections (for installation and updates)

For all technical support queries (including no CD drive), please phone Scholastic Customer Services on 0845 6039091.

Designed using Adobe Indesign
Scholastic Education, an imprint of Scholastic Ltd
Book End, Range Road, Witney, Oxfordshire, OX29 0YD
Registered office: Westfield Road, Southam, Warwickshire CV47 0RA

Printed and bound by Ashford Colour Press
© 2016 Scholastic Ltd
1 2 3 4 5 6 7 8 9   6 7 8 9 0 1 2 3 4 5

British Library Cataloguing-in-Publication Data
A catalogue record for this book is available from the British Library.
ISBN 978-1407-16062-7

Due to the nature of the web, we cannot guarantee the content or links of any site mentioned. We strongly recommend that teachers check websites before using them in the classroom.

Author Samantha Pope
Editorial team Rachel Morgan, Jenny Wilcox, Margaret Eaton and Vicky Butt
Series designer Neil Salt
Designer Anna Oliwa
Illustrator Eric Smith/Beehive Illustration
Digital development Hannah Barnett, Phil Crothers and MWA Technologies Private Ltd

Acknowledgements
Every effort has been made to trace copyright holders for the works reproduced in this book, and the publishers apologise for any inadvertent omissions.

CONTENTS

Introduction 4

Using the CD-ROM 5

Curriculum links 6

About the book and author 8

Guided reading 9

Shared reading 13

Grammar, punctuation & spelling 19

Plot, character & setting 25

Talk about it 32

Get writing 38

Assessment 44

▼ INTRODUCTION

Read & Respond provides teaching ideas related to a specific children's book. The series focuses on best-loved books and brings you ways to use them to engage your class and enthuse them about reading.

The book is divided into different sections:

- **About the book and author:** gives you some background information about the book and the author.

- **Guided reading:** breaks the book down into sections and gives notes for using it with guided reading groups. A bookmark has been provided on page 12 containing comprehension questions. The children can be directed to refer to these as they read.

- **Shared reading:** provides extracts from the children's book with associated notes for focused work. There is also one non-fiction extract that relates to the children's book.

- **Grammar, punctuation & spelling:** provides word-level work related to the children's book so you can teach grammar, punctuation and spelling in context.

- **Plot, character & setting:** contains activity ideas focused on the plot, characters and the setting of the story.

- **Talk about it:** has speaking and listening activities related to the children's book. These activities may be based directly on the children's book or be broadly based on the themes and concepts of the story.

- **Get writing:** provides writing activities related to the children's book. These activities may be based directly on the children's book or be broadly based on the themes and concepts of the story.

- **Assessment:** contains short activities that will help you assess whether the children have understood concepts and curriculum objectives. They are designed to be informal activities to feed into your planning.

The activities follow the same format:

- **Objective:** the objective for the lesson. It will be based upon a curriculum objective, but will often be more specific to the focus being covered.

- **What you need:** a list of resources you need to teach the lesson, including digital resources (printable pages, interactive activities and media resources, see page 5).

- **What to do:** the activity notes.

- **Differentiation:** this is provided where specific and useful differentiation advice can be given to support and/or extend the learning in the activity. Differentiation by providing additional adult support has not been included as this will be at a teacher's discretion based upon specific children's needs and ability, as well as the availability of support.

The activities are numbered for reference within each section and should move through the text sequentially – so you can use the lesson while you are reading the book. Once you have read the book, most of the activities can be used in any order you wish.

Below are brief guidance notes for using the CD-ROM. For more detailed information, please click on the '?' button in the top right-hand corner of the screen.

The program contains the following:
- the extract pages from the book
- all of the photocopiable pages from the book
- additional printable pages
- interactive on-screen activities
- media resources.

Getting started

Put the CD-ROM into your CD-ROM drive. If you do not have a CD-ROM drive, phone Scholastic Customer Services on 0845 6039091.

- For Windows users, the install wizard should autorun. If it fails to do so then navigate to your CD-ROM drive and follow the installation process.
- For Mac users, copy the disk image file to your hard drive. After it has finished copying double click it to mount the disk image. Navigate to the mounted disk image and run the installer. After installation the disk image can be unmounted and the DMG can be deleted from the hard drive.
- To install on a network, see the ReadMe file located on the CD-ROM (navigate to your drive).

To complete the installation of the program you need to open the program and click 'Update' in the pop-up. Please note – this CD-ROM is web-enabled and the content will be downloaded from the internet to your hard drive to populate the CD-ROM with the relevant resources. This only needs to be done on first use. After this you will be able to use the CD-ROM without an internet connection. If at any point any content is updated, you will receive another pop-up upon start up when there is an internet connection.

Main menu

The main menu is the first screen that appears. Here you can access: terms and conditions, registration links, how to use the CD-ROM and credits. To access a specific book click on the relevant button (Note only titles installed will be available). You can filter by the

drop-down lists if you wish. You can search all resources by clicking 'Search' in the bottom left-hand corner. You can also log in and access favourites that you have bookmarked.

Resources

By clicking on a book on the Main menu, you are taken to the resources for that title. The resources are: Media, Interactives, Extracts and Printables. Select the category and then launch a resource by clicking the play button.

Teacher settings

In the top right-hand corner of the screen is a small 'T' icon. This is the teacher settings area. It is password protected. The password is: login. This area will allow you to choose the print quality settings for interactive activities ('Default' or 'Best') and also allow you to check for updates to the program or re-download all content to the disk via 'Refresh all content'. You can also set up user logins so that you can save and access favourites. Once a user is set up, they can enter by clicking the login link underneath the 'T' and '?' buttons.

Search

You can access an all resources search by clicking the search button on the bottom left of the Main menu. You can search for activities by type (using the drop-down filter) or by keyword by typing into the box. You can then assign resources to your favourites area or launch them directly from the search area.

CURRICULUM LINKS

Section	Activity	Curriculum objectives
Guided reading		Comprehension: To develop positive attitudes to reading and understanding of what they read.
Shared reading	1	Comprehension: To ask questions to improve their understanding of a text.
	2	Comprehension: To draw inferences such as inferring characters' feelings, thoughts and motives from their actions, and justifying inferences with evidence.
	3	Comprehension: To check that the text makes sense to them, discussing their understanding and explaining the meaning of words in context.
	4	Comprehension: To identify how language, structure and presentation contribute to meaning.
Grammar, punctuation & spelling	1	Transcription: To place the possessive apostrophe accurately in words with regular and irregular plurals.
	2	Transcription: To use further prefixes and suffixes and understand how to add them.
	3	Composition: To extend the range of sentences with more than one clause by using a wider range of conjunctions, including 'when', 'if', 'because', 'although'.
	4	Word reading: To apply their growing knowledge of root words, prefixes and suffixes both to read aloud and to understand the meaning of new words they meet.
	5	Transcription: To spell further homophones.
	6	Composition: To use and punctuate direct speech; to use commas after fronted adverbials.
Plot, character & setting	1	Comprehension: To use dictionaries to check the meaning of words that they have read.
	2	Comprehension: To identify themes and conventions in a wide range of books.
	3	Comprehension: To identify main ideas drawn from more than one paragraph and summarise these.
	4	Comprehension: To identify how language, structure and presentation contribute to meaning.
	5	Comprehension: To draw inferences such as inferring characters' feelings, thoughts and motives from their actions, and justifying inferences with evidence.
	6	Comprehension: To ask questions to improve their understanding of a text. Spoken language: To participate in role play.
	7	Comprehension: To prepare poems and play scripts to read aloud and to perform, showing understanding through intonation, tone, volume and action.

Section	Activity	Curriculum objectives
Talk about it	1	Spoken language: To consider and evaluate different viewpoints, attending to and building on the contribution of others.
	2	Spoken language: To participate in role play.
	3	Spoken language: To articulate and justify answers, arguments and opinions.
	4	Spoken language: To participate in presentations.
	5	Spoken language: To develop understanding through speculating, hypothesising, and imagining and exploring ideas.
	6	Spoken language: To participate in role play.
Get writing	1	Composition: To discuss writing similar to that which they are planning to write in order to understand and learn from its structure, vocabulary and grammar.
	2	Composition: To assess the effectiveness of their own and others' writing and suggest improvements.
	3	Composition: To create settings, characters and plot.
	4	Composition: To discuss and record ideas.
	5	Composition: To organise paragraphs around a theme.
	6	Composition: To use simple organisational devices in non-narrative material.
Assessment	1	Composition: To indicate possession by using the possessive apostrophe with plural nouns.
	2	Word reading: To apply their growing knowledge of root words, prefixes and suffixes, both to read aloud and to understand the meaning of new words they meet.
	3	Comprehension: To check that the text makes sense to them, discussing their understanding and explaining the meaning of words in context.
	4	Transcription: To use further prefixes and suffixes and understand how to add them.
	5	Transcription: To spell further homophones.
	6	Comprehension: To increase their familiarity with a wide range of books.

About the book

What would you do if you thought that God had dropped a bag of money from the sky especially for you? Brothers Damian and Anthony are excited… but they can't agree on what to do with it. Damian wants to give it away to good causes, while Anthony thinks they should spend it on themselves. As they start trying to get rid of it just days before the euro replaces the pound, people start noticing that the boys are suddenly rich… and they want to get in on the cash. Soon everyone at school has money, either from selling or lending their things or for doing favours. However, as Damian and Anthony discover, the more money that's around, the less it's worth.

But *Millions* is about much more than having loads of money. Damian and Anthony have just moved house, and school, and they are trying to adapt to life without their mum. Damian copes with his grief over her death by becoming a walking encyclopaedia on saints, while Anthony obsesses about property. Their hardworking father encourages them to be good and strive for excellence, and Damian in particular takes this to heart, but not always in the right way.

After Damian makes an unusually large donation to Water Aid at school, suspicions are raised. Dorothy, the speaker, tries to get to know the family better but Anthony doesn't trust her motives. Will she break their trust and hearts?

Originally, Frank Cottrell Boyce wrote *Millions* as a screenplay for a film by the same name but then adapted it and turned it into a novel. The book was published in February 2004, and the film was released in cinemas six months later.

About the author

Frank Cottrell Boyce was born in 1959 in Liverpool. He studied for a first degree in English at Keble College, Oxford, followed by a doctorate, also at Oxford University.

Cottrell Boyce has had a long and successful writing career. He has worked for magazines, written screenplays for films, and was even a writer on the popular soap opera *Coronation Street*. More recently, he was the writer for the opening ceremony at the 2012 Olympic Games in London with a theme based on Shakespeare's 'The Tempest'.

His books for children have proved very popular. *Millions* was his first book, published in 2004, followed by *Framed* (2005) and *Cosmic* (2008). *The Unforgotten Coat* (2011) was commissioned by a charity and he also wrote *Chitty Chitty Bang Bang Flies Again* – a sequel to Ian Fleming's original book. His most recent novel, *The Astounding Broccoli Boy*, was published in 2015.

Frank Cottrell Boyce is married and has seven children.

Key facts

Millions

Author: Frank Cottrell Boyce

First published: 2004 by Macmillan Children's Books

Awards: The book won the prestigious CILIP Carnegie Medal in 2004, an annual award given by British librarians for the best children's book published in the UK. It was also shortlisted for the 2005 Branford Boase Award (which is given to a first-time writer of a children's or young adult's novel), the Guardian Children's Fiction Prize and the Blue Peter Book Award.

Considering the covers

Start by asking the children to look at the front cover. Ask: *What do the illustrations show, and what do they tell you about the book?* (They show a young boy looking worried or confused and carrying a bag of money against the background of a giant male figure.) *Why is there a circle around the giant's head?* (This is possibly because he's meant to be a saint but, if so, why does he look threatening?)

Look at question 1 on the Guided Reading bookmark (page 12). Explain to the children that the subtitle 'the not-so-great train robbery' might perhaps be because it doesn't turn out well for the robbers who stole the money originally.

Turn to the back cover and point out the four questions that precede the main blurb. Ask the children why they are there. (To make the readers speculate on what the book is about.) Do they make the children want to read the book?

Does the blurb underneath cover the main themes of the book, in their opinion? (There is no right or wrong answer, but while it covers the main plot device, it doesn't mention all the philosophical issues the book covers.) Ask: *Why is there no mention of Damian's mum's death?* (It might put people off by giving the impression that this is a sad book.)

Finally, ask the children if the short quotations from reviews make them want to read the book, or do they make no difference at all.

Chapter 1

In Chapter 1, we meet our narrator, Damian, who suggests that the story he is about to tell would be different if his brother were narrating it instead. Refer to question 9 on the bookmark and discuss the children's responses.

Next, ask: *Why has Damian dedicated the story to St Francis of Assisi?* (Like Damian, he stole money to give to the poor) *Does this give any clues as to what the book is about and what Damian is like as a character?*

Ask the children if they think Damian is wise to talk about a saint as a person he admires, rather than a footballer, especially on his first day at a new school. Would they want to be friends with him? Then discuss question 2 on the bookmark. Explain that the children possibly drew violent pictures because they loved the gruesome details given by Damian!

Refer the children to question 8 on the bookmark and discuss as a class. Ask: *Why do people react the way they do when they hear about the boys' mother being dead?* (They feel awkward and don't know what to say.)

Chapters 2–7

Ask the children to summarise Damian's and Anthony's different attitudes towards money. (Anthony is fascinated by it, whereas Damian doesn't care about money: 'Personally, I think, so what? Money's just a thing and things change.') Which opinion do the children share more – Anthony's or Damian's?

Damian puts the holly under his shirt to be more saint-like. Ask the children: *Why do you think Mr Quinn was worried about this? Would you be worried if you were Damian's dad or teacher?*

See if the children know where Damian went with his dad (a special mental health place for children). Ask: *Why was his father angry after the session?* (He's worried about Damian's behaviour.) Anthony tells Damian he was sent there because 'they think you're bonkers'. Is he right?

In Chapter 5, we find out a little more about Damian's mum and her death. Refer to question 3 on the bookmark: *Why weren't the adults honest with Damian and Anthony about what was happening with their mother?* (They were probably trying to avoid upsetting them.) *Do you think that the adults should have been more open? Why?*

At the end of Chapter 8, the money lands in Damian's hermitage, and he thinks it's a gift from God. Ask: *Why is that?* (He told God that his mother was dead, and Anthony says that this makes people give things to them.)

Chapters 8–12

These chapters focus on the effect the money has on the children at the school. Ask the class: *Would you pay someone to queue for your school dinner? Or for extra helpings of pudding?*

Damian calls the school playground 'one big car-boot sale'. Ask: *What does he mean by that?* (The children were bringing in used stuff from home to sell and people were bargaining for it.)

Ask: *Why can't Damian and Anthony tell their dad about the money?* (Damian has wanted to from the start but Anthony tries to stop him, perhaps because he knows that their father will be honest and insist that they turn the money in to the police.)

In Chapter 9, Anthony says it would be 'impractical' to give money to the poor because it would be hard to find them where they live. Look at question 7 on the bookmark and ask: *What does Anthony mean by 'the only people who can afford to live here are nice people'?* (He seems to be saying that poor people aren't nice!)

At the end of Chapter 10, Damian asks: 'What if giving people money just makes people more money-ish?' Refer to question 10 on the bookmark and discuss the children's responses.

In Chapter 11, Damian's hermitage is trashed. While Saint Charles Lwanga helps him tidy it up, he says that water is more valuable than money in places like Uganda. Shortly after this, Dorothy gives a presentation in school about the charity Water Aid. Refer the children to question 5 on the bookmark and discuss their responses to the questions raised.

After Damian makes a huge donation to Water Aid, Anthony decides to show him a website describing where the money originally came from. Ask the children why he does this. (He feared Damian would cause trouble spending large amounts of money like that.)

Ask: *Why did Anthony lie to the school about them stealing the money from the Mormons?* (He didn't want to say where the money came from as he wanted to keep the rest. He knew if he blamed their actions on their mother's death that they would be let off the hook.) *Why did the Mormons agree with Anthony's lie?* (They wanted more money.) *What does Damian think about this?* (He is upset because they aren't acting like proper saints.)

Chapters 13–20

Dorothy comes into the boys' life from this point onwards and everyone acts differently. Ask: *How does Damian's father react?* (He's happier and watches 'Who Wants to be a Millionnaire?' for the first time since the mother died.) *Why is Anthony so rude to her?* (He doesn't trust her as he thinks that she is after their money. He is also worried that she might take his mother's place and will break their father's heart.)

Dorothy tells Damian that she only does charity

work 'for whoever pays… If I won a million I'd put it in the bank and never shake a tin again.' Ask the children why Damian is disappointed by Dorothy's admission. (He probably hoped she shared his desire to do good.) Then refer them to question 11 on the bookmark. Point out that adults often see a job as a job and don't necessarily do things to help others.

In Chapter 14, Damian meets St Peter. Ask: *Is St Peter portrayed in a saint-like way?* (No – he swears a lot and talks about stress.) Do they think St Peter really did give Damian the key to his old house?

After Damian's dad rescues him from their old house, Anthony and Damian tell him about the money. Ask: *Why do they do this now?* (Anthony is struggling to keep the money a secret and to know what to do with it.)

Damian's father was going to hand over the money to the police, but when he discovers his house was burgled, he changes his mind. Refer to question 4 on the bookmark. Explain that Damian's dad always does the right thing and it led to him being burgled. He feels fed up with the world and decides to break the rules for a change.

In Chapter 16, Glass Eye turns up and tells Damian what to do with the money. Ask: *Why doesn't Damian tell his father?* (He might have been too scared of the consequences. But also, he says that he feels Glass Eye is the only person who understood, like him, the burden of having the money.)

When Dorothy disappears with the money, why does everyone think that she has gone for good? (She told Damian to shush before she left, and she's turned her phone off.) Ask the children: *Did you think she had gone too?*

Damian, Dorothy, Anthony and Dad spend the day in Manchester trying to change the money into euros

before the deadline. Up until this point, Damian has been very honest with the money but now he is helping Dorothy by pretending to need the loo to get out of difficult situations. Discuss question 6 on the bookmark with the children.

When the family is celebrating, Anthony suddenly gets upset and says to Damian: 'Hear that? He'll be laughing on the other side of his face when she goes and leaves him, won't he? Remember what he was like when Mum went.' Refer to question 12 on the bookmark. Explain that the implication is that their father had been very upset – perhaps Anthony had to help him deal with his emotions.

When Damian burns the money at the end of the book, he sees his mother and says: 'I know you're only a dream but I don't care. It's nice to see you, even in a dream.' Ask the children: *Why does Damian say that this is a dream whereas he seemed to believe in the saints' visits?* (Perhaps he thinks this is too good to be true. Or maybe he knows that he sees things.)

The story ends like the beginning, with Damian commenting about how the story would be different if it were Anthony narrating it. Do the children agree with this? How would it be different? Does Anthony really regret them giving the money away?

SCHOLASTIC
READ & RESPOND
Bringing the best books to life in the classroom

Millions
By Frank Cottrell Boyce

Focus on...
Meaning

1. Why is the book's subtitle: 'the not-so-great train robbery'?

2. Why did the children all draw violent pictures after they heard what Damian said about the saints?

3. Why weren't the adults honest with Damian and Anthony about what was happening with their mother?

4. Why did Damian's dad decide not to tell the police about the money?

Focus on...
Organisation

5. Does the author include St Charles Lwanga's visit to Damian before Dorothy's visit to the school to suggest that the saints are playing a part in Damian's life? Or is it a coincidence?

6. Why is Damian now helping to deceive others? What is the author trying to say?

SCHOLASTIC
READ & RESPOND
Bringing the best books to life in the classroom

Millions
By Frank Cottrell Boyce

Focus on...
Language and features

7. What does Anthony mean by 'the only people who can afford to live here are nice people'?

8. How can Anthony speak so bluntly about his mother's death when he tries to get things? Why doesn't he get upset?

Focus on...
Purpose, viewpoints and effects

9. Whose version of events do you think would be most interesting – Damian's or Anthony's?

10. Do you think Damian's question reflects one of the author's main themes of the book?

11. What might the author be saying about the choices adults make in their working life?

12. What is the author telling us about how Damian's and Anthony's dad reacted to their mum's death?

Extract 1

- Display and read aloud Extract 1 on the interactive whiteboard. This extract is from Chapter 10.

- Ask the children: *What are the warning signs that Barry is getting angry?* (The detailed description of his eye and how it flutters.) *Why does Barry get so angry about being asked if he is poor?* (Barry might think Damian is insulting him, or maybe Barry is poor but doesn't want people knowing or commenting on it.)

- Ask the children if they think Barry had a good reason to beat up Damian if he thought Damian was insulting him. Why or why not?

- Why does Barry think that wearing Rockports is a sign that he is not poor? (They are expensive and fashionable shoes.) Ask: *Is it possible to own expensive clothes and shoes if you don't have much money? How could Barry afford the shoes?* (Everyone in the school now had money because of Anthony and Damian.)

- Damian seems pleased at the outcome of the episode. What proof in the text can children find to support this? (Damian calls suffering persecution 'just fantastic' and talks about 'five rungs'.) Ask: *When Damian refers to rungs, what does he mean?* (He thinks that any form of suffering will take him higher on the ladder to heaven.) *Do you think that Damian is acting entirely unselfishly?* (The children might think this, but they could also argue that if Damian is using these events to get closer to heaven, he is acting with an ulterior motive.)

- The extract ends with Anthony's explanation of why Damian feels 'a bit floaty' (the side effects of being beaten up). Ask the children what effect this has on Damian's version of events. (It makes the possibility of Damian having a heavenly experience funny and unlikely.)

Extract 2

- Display and read out Extract 2 from Chapter 12 to the children, considering the following points, and inviting debate and opinion.

- Ask: *When Anthony reveals where the money has really come from, how does Damian react?* (He's angry/upset.) *How can you tell?* (Damian shouts at Anthony to shut up several times – being angry is unusual for Damian.)

- Ask the children why Damian is so angry. (He wants to believe that God was responsible.) *Do you think that Damian really believed that the money came from God? Why?* (This will depend on each child's response to the text. They may think that he did as he is so obsessed with saints and heaven throughout the book. They might suggest that, deep down, he knows it was from somewhere else but needed to believe in an act of God to believe in heaven, otherwise where is his mum?)

- Ask: *If Anthony already knew about where the money came from, why is he telling Damian now?* (He is starting to panic as Damian's spending is drawing attention to the large sum of money that they have.) Do the children think he should have been honest with Damian before?

- Ask: *How does Anthony try to convince Damian that they have to be careful?* (He talks at length about the kind of people who might be after the money, and what they might do when they can't find it.)

- Ask: *In the long paragraph, why does Anthony use so many questions?* (He uses rhetorical questions – ones that don't need an answer – to try to emphasise how serious the situation is. He asks the questions he thinks Damian should be asking but might not. He knows Damian must understand what is at stake.)

Extract 3

- With the class, read Extract 3 from Chapter 13 (or invite three volunteers to come up and read the parts of the three different speakers).

- Ask: *Do you think Anthony likes Dorothy? How can you tell?* (Most children will pick up on the fact that he doesn't like her. Evidence of this is in his short, blunt answers to her and his insistence that they can manage the washing up on their own.)

- Ask: *Why doesn't Anthony like Dorothy?* (He might be suspicious that she's after the money. He might be frightened of someone taking the place of his mother, even though he never talks about his feelings about her death.)

- Ask: *What do you think Dorothy is trying to do in this scene?* (She seems keen to get on with the boys and excited to be part of the family.) Do the children think her interest is genuine?

- Tell the children you'd like to take a look at the author's use of figurative language in this extract. Ask them if they can find examples of a simile and a metaphor. (Simile: 'Dorothy lit up like a Christmas decoration'; metaphor: 'The light went off inside her'.) Circle these on the board and ask the children what impression these give about Dorothy. (A lit Christmas decoration is bright and cheerful, which reflects her happiness and excitement. When the light goes out, Dorothy loses her happiness and sparkle.) Ask: *Do the simile and metaphor work well here?*

- Ask: *What do you think Dad feels about what is happening?* (He seems to be warning Anthony to be quiet when Anthony rejects offers of help with the washing up.) *How does Dad feel towards Dorothy?* (It would suggest that he likes her and wants Anthony to be nice.)

Extract 4

- Ask if any of the children knows how a person becomes a saint. If anyone does, they might summarise by saying that the person must be dead and have performed a miracle or lived a good life, all of which is true. However, there are a few more details to be aware of!

- Display Extract 4 on the interactive whiteboard and read through the text, which gives details about the steps taken to canonise a person.

- Ask the children: *Can you think of examples of how a person might live a good or holy life? What things might they do?* (Answers could include: regular attendance at church, charity work, helping people who are ill or sad, praying, talking to other people about God, and so on.)

- Ask for opinions on the process of becoming a saint. Do the children think that it should take so long? Is it too hard?

- Ask the children if they know of any miracles performed by saints. (They might list any that they read in the book). Do they know what a miracle is? (It is anything that helps a person or a being or a situation without any logical explanation about how it happened. Often a miracle concerns someone's health – a person could make a miraculous recovery when they were diagnosed as dying, for example.)

- Ask: *If you could perform one miracle in the world, what would it be?* Discuss the children's responses.

Extract 1

Chapter 10

It was the wink that put the thought in my head. I thought, Hello, is this another rung? And I said, 'Barry, are you poor?'

Barry's left eyelid had still not come up from its wink. Now it fluttered a bit, then it opened wide, wide, wide and stared into mine.

'What?'

'Are you poor?'

He hit me very hard across the face. I remembered to turn the other cheek. He hit me in the stomach. I had to sit on the floor to get my breath back. He put his shoe next to my face and said, 'See that shoe? What does it say on it?'

It said, Rockport.

'Would I have Rockports if I was poor?' And then he kicked me and I couldn't breathe for what seemed like a long weekend.

Now this might sound like it wasn't that successful, but that depends how you look at it. It's true I didn't help a poor person but I did try, so that's got to be worth a rung, and, more importantly, I did suffer persecution, which is just fantastic. I mean, five rungs at least. In fact, as I was lying on the tarmac, I actually did start to feel a bit floaty, like I might rise up into Heaven. Anthony said that this was due to a change in air pressure inside my head caused by the loss of blood from my nose.

Extract 2

Chapter 12

At first I couldn't think of anything to say. Then I said, 'Shut up!'

'What?'

'What did you have to go and do that for? Why couldn't you keep it to yourself?'

'Damian…'

'I saw it. It fell out of the sky.'

'You saw it fall off the back of a train.'

'Shut up! Shut up! Shut up! Why d'you have to tell me?'

'Because you need to know. Because the people who did this, they're dangerous. They dropped the money all over the country. So there must be dozens of them. If one of them was supposed to collect a bag and got there late, what would happen then? Someone else might have found it. Someone like you. D'you think they'd just say, oh dear, never mind? Or d'you think they'd go looking for it? They'd come looking for it, Damian, looking for you, and they could be anyone – a man with a glass eye, a woman with corn rows, some people with funny accents and unfeasibly white shirts. You've got to be careful. They'll want their money back and they'll want it quick. They've only got a few days left to change it.'

'I thought it came from God.'

'What?'

'Who else would have that much cash?'

'Well, maybe it did. After all, God does move in mysterious ways.'

Extract 3

Chapter 13

When we'd all finished, Dorothy looked at her watch and said, 'I'm much later than I planned. But I can't go without helping you to wash up.'

Anthony said, 'No, no. We don't mind washing up. We do it every night. If you've got to go, you…'

Dad stopped him. 'Anthony,' he said.

'What?'

Dad looked at him for a second, as if he was trying to work something out, and then he said, 'What *is* in your school bag, by the way. Can't all be homework.'

It could have been a dangerous moment, but Anthony had had time to think now. 'It's sort of homework. It's costumes. For the nativity play.'

Dorothy lit up like a Christmas decoration. 'Nativity play!' she said, 'I haven't seen a nativity play for years. What are you? The kings? Are you going to let us have a look? Go on, go and get them. Give us a treat.'

'No.'

The light went off inside her.

Extract 4

How to become a saint

It's not easy to become a saint – as Damian shows in Millions, a lot is required of a person before they can reach such an honoured position. So how do you get to put those coveted two letters – St – before your name?

You can't be alive

The basic requirement is that you must have been dead for at least five years before you can even be considered. This allows enough time to pass for people to make an unemotional judgement based on their reaction to your death.

You have to perform miracles

Before you can be called a saint, you must perform a miracle based on prayers people have made to you after you died. If their prayers come true, this is proof that you are in heaven and can talk to God on other people's behalf. You can now be called 'blessed'.

But now you need a second miracle, based on prayers coming true, in order to be declared a proper saint (unless you are a martyr, in which case you only need one miracle). Once this is achieved, you will become a saint through the canonisation process.

You must have proof

Your local bishop will decide whether you should be put forth as a saint. He will look for proof that you've behaved in a holy and virtuous manner when alive, and will ask for proof from people who knew you (since you are dead). Good evidence includes inspiring people to prayer through your actions.

If you are holy enough, the bishop will ask for you to be recommended to the Pope, who is the head of the Roman Catholic Church. He's responsible for making a person a saint (Popes are always male, never female). If he agrees that you have lived a life of 'heroic virtue' he will allow you to be called 'venerable'.

GRAMMAR, PUNCTUATION & SPELLING

1. Punctuate possessively

Objective

To place the possessive apostrophe in regular and irregular plurals.

What you need

Media resource 'Possessive apostrophes', interactive activity 'Punctuate possessively', photocopiable page 22 'Who does it belong to?'.

What to do

- Ask the children how to make a regular noun plural (you add an 's') and invite them to give you some examples ('chairs', 'girls', 'boys', 'pets', 'oranges', 'houses' and so on). Then see if they can think of any irregular plural nouns. (Suggestions could include 'women', 'men', 'witches', 'babies', 'geese', 'classes'.)

- Tell the children that they are going to work on possessive adjectives in singular and plural nouns, both regular and irregular. Display media resource 'Possessive apostrophes' and go through the text with the class, explaining anything that is unclear.

- Then open interactive activity 'Punctuate possessively'. Ask: *Where does the apostrophe go in the singular nouns?* Invite volunteers to come up to type the answers into the boxes provided. Then ask them to put the nouns into their plural possessive form in the second half of the activity.

- Finally, ask the children to complete photocopiable page 22 'Who does it belong to?'.

Differentiation

Support: Children who find this difficult could focus on learning the plurals of regular nouns instead. You could write these on the board and ask the children to write the plurals on an individual whiteboard or piece of paper. Sample words could include: 'table', 'desk', 'pen', 'paper', 'pencil', 'shoe', 'bag'.

2. Super suffixes

Objective

To add the suffix 'ly'.

What you need

Media resource 'Forming adverbs', interactive activity 'Super suffixes'.

What to do

- Start the lesson by recapping what a suffix is (letters that go onto the end of a root word, which either change or add to its meaning).

- Ask the children if they can think of any examples of suffixes that do not need any changes to the root word. Suggestions could include words that end in 'ed', 'ing', 'er', 'est' such as 'jumped', 'jumping', 'taller', 'tallest'.

- They may also remember words that need an extra letter before the suffix is added, such as 'spotted', 'sadder', 'saddest', 'batting', 'hitting'.

- Now display the media resource 'Forming adverbs'. Go through the rules of adding the 'ly' suffix to adjectives to form adverbs. Ask for some examples and write these on the whiteboard. Then go through the exceptions with the class, inviting further examples if desired.

- Open the interactive activity 'Super suffixes'. Invite volunteers to come to the whiteboard to type the correct 'ly' adverb next to the corresponding adjective in the list shown on the screen.

- On the following screen, the most suitable adverb has to be selected from the options contained in each drop-down box. Again, invite volunteers to do this, encouraging them to justify their choice each time.

Differentiation

Support: Let children concentrate on simple 'ly' suffixes only.

3. Clever conjunctions

Objective

To extend the range of sentences with more than one clause, using 'when', 'if', 'because', 'although'.

What you need

Media resource 'Using conjunctions', interactive activity 'Clever conjunctions', photocopiable page 23 'When, if, because, although...'.

What to do

- To begin, see if the children can tell you what a conjunction is (a word that joins together two words or clauses, or two simple sentences, into one longer one). Ask for some examples, writing the children's suggestions on the whiteboard.

- Next, ask why conjunctions are useful in sentences (for example, they make sentences longer and more interesting – writing would look very odd and boring if it were only made up of short sentences). Can the children give you some examples of sentences containing conjunctions? Write some of their suggestions on the board.

- Display the media resource 'Using conjunctions' and read through the rules with the children.

- Then open the interactive activity 'Clever conjunctions'. Invite volunteers to come up to the front of the class to highlight the conjunctions in the sentences displayed on the screen.

- Finally, provide each child with a copy of photocopiable page 23 'When, if, because, although...'. Ask them to create their own sentences, using two conjunctions in each sentence. This could either be done in class or as homework.

Differentiation

Support: Children who find the activity on the photocopiable sheet difficult could focus on writing sentences with just one conjunction instead.

4. Perfect prefixes

Objective

To apply knowledge of prefixes to understand the meaning of new words.

What you need

Media resource 'Adding prefixes', interactive activity 'Perfect prefixes'.

What to do

- Start off by revising what a prefix is with the class (letters or a word that you add on to the beginning of a word to change its meaning). Ask: *Can anyone give me an example of words that contain a prefix?* Answers might include: 'impossible', 'misbehave', 'superman', 'autograph'.

- Display media resource 'Adding prefixes'. With the children, read through the rules for adding different prefixes, including the exceptions. Check that they understand the explanations.

- Next, open interactive activity 'Perfect prefixes'. For screen 1, invite volunteers to come to the whiteboard to drag the lines across to join each prefix to its meaning.

- On the following screen the children are required to drag the correct prefix to the word it precedes. Again, ask for volunteers (different children this time if possible) to have a go (tell them that in some cases more than one prefix may be acceptable).

Differentiation

Support: Ask less confident learners to focus on fewer prefixes. Try giving them the following words to add the correct prefix: '(im)possible', '(un)ripe', '(mis)behave', '(dis)believe'.

Extension: Ask children to write down the following headings: 'super', 're', 'inter', 'anti', 'auto', 'sub'. Challenge them to find as many words with these prefixes as possible for each one.

5. Hearing homophones

Objective

To use homophones in the correct context.

What you need

Interactive activity 'There, their or they're?', photocopiable page 24 'Hearing homophones'.

What to do

- Ask: *Do you know what homophones are?* (Two or more words that sound the same but are spelled differently, and mean different things.) *Can you give me some examples?* If the children find this difficult, write some examples on the whiteboard ('knight/ night', 'see/sea', 'brake/break', 'flower/flour'...). See if they can then suggest any more possibilities.

- Next, open the interactive activity 'There, their or they're?'. Before they start the activity, remind the children about these rules:
  - **they're** is short for **they are**
  - **there** refers to a place, where you might find something
  - **their** means that something belongs to someone.

- Now invite volunteers to come up to choose the correct form of 'there', 'their' or 'they're' from each drop-down menu to complete the sentences.

- Finally, provide each child with photocopiable page 24 'Hearing homophones'. Read out each sentence twice – once for them to hear it and once for them to write their answers. (The missing words that you should include as you read out each sentence are (1) there, (2) hear, (3) too, (4) see, (5) night, (6) grown, (7) write, (8) he'll.) When they have completed this, check their answers and explain anything that is difficult.

Differentiation

Support: Give children a list of the missing words on the photocopiable sheet. Then all they need do is put them in the right place.
Extension: Challenge children to write sentences using their own homophones.

6. Dashing dialogue

Objective

To punctuate direct speech; to use commas after fronted adverbials.

What you need

Media resource 'Writing dialogue', interactive activity 'Dashing dialogue'.

What to do

- Tell the children that in this lesson they will be focusing on how to use appropriate punctuation when writing dialogue.

- Open media resource 'Writing dialogue' which gives simple instructions on how to punctuate dialogue in written work. Go through each of the points with the children, checking that they understand each rule before moving on to the next one. To consolidate their learning, you could ask the children to give you their own examples. You may also wish to spend a little more time explaining fronted adverbials and their role in sentences, asking for or giving examples.

- Now open interactive activity 'Dashing dialogue'. This displays an imaginary dialogue between Anthony and Damian. The children need to drag and drop the correct punctuation into the blank boxes to complete each sentence (the draggable tiles can be used more than once).

- You could either do this as a whole-class activity, or you could ask children to work in pairs, discussing what punctuation they would use, and then inviting a child from each pair to drag and drop one or more punctuation marks into place.

Differentiation

Support: Let children omit the fronted adverbials and concentrate on the opening and closing punctuation marks only.
Extension: Challenge children to write their own made-up dialogue, using the punctuation marks correctly.

Who does it belong to?

● The sentences below have mistakes in them. Turn the emboldened nouns into their correct possessive spelling. Write the corrected noun in the space provided on the right.

1. **Damians** hermitage is by the railway tracks.

2. The **saints** names are interesting.

3. **Anthonys** main interest is in property.

4. The **mens** TV is brand new.

5. The **womens** make-up looks false.

6. The **childrens** wealth is increasing.

7. **St Peters** opinions are surprising.

8. The **shopkeepers** surprise is obvious.

When, if, because, although...

● Write five sentences, using two of the following conjunctions in each one: when, if, because, although.

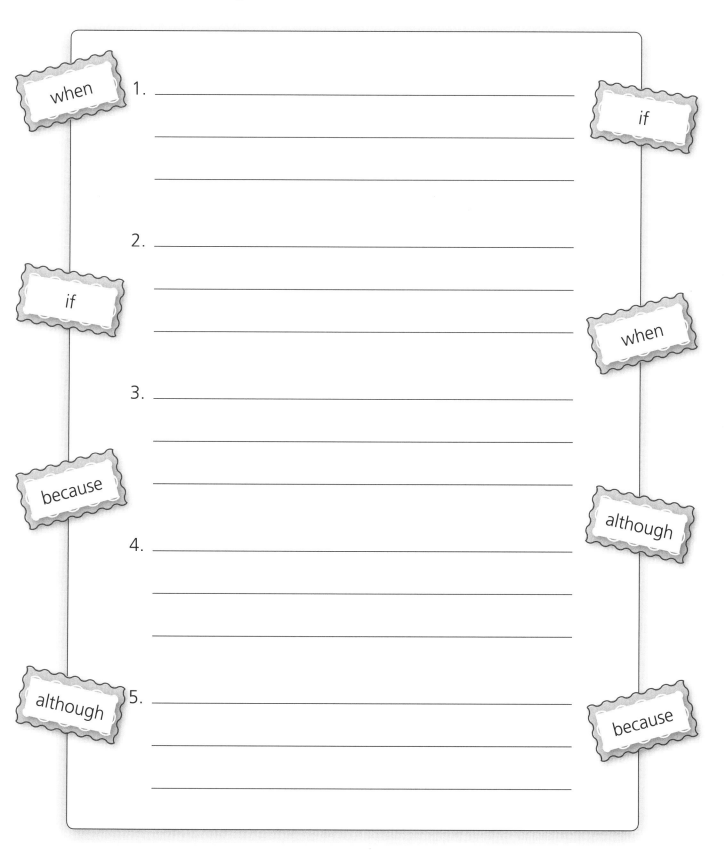

when

if

1. _____

_____

_____

2. _____

if

when

_____

_____

3. _____

because

although

_____

_____

4. _____

_____

_____

_____

although

because

5. _____

_____

_____

Hearing homophones

● First, listen carefully as your teacher reads out the sentences below. When your teacher reads them a second time, fill in the gaps with the correct homophone (the context will help you).

1. Once upon a time, _____ was a boy called Damian.

2. He could _____ saints.

3. Sometimes, he could see them _____.

4. But the one saint he wanted to _____ never came.

5. The best _____ was when he finally spoke to his Mum.

6. He knew he'd remember it when he was _____ up.

7. Damian believes that if Anthony were to _____ the story, it would be different.

8. He isn't happy about the money but _____ get over it.

1. Word detectives

Objective

To use a dictionary to check the meaning of words.

What you need

Copies of *Millions,* dictionaries, photocopiable page 29 'Word detectives'.

What to do

- Tell the children that they are going to be 'word detectives', using dictionaries to help them find out the meanings of unusual words.

- Explain that Damian uses a lot of special and unusual words in *Millions*, particularly concerning religion. Ask: *Can anyone give me an example of a religious word that Damian uses?* (Children might mention (patron) saint, martyr, hermitage, persecution.) If they do give you any examples, see if they can give you a definition of the word.

- Next, hand out photocopiable page 29 'Word detectives'. Explain that the sheet contains some of the religious words that Damian uses when talking about the saints and himself. Ask the children, either alone or in pairs, to look up each word in the dictionary and then write a short meaning next to it. Once they have done this, they should try to use it in a sentence of their own creation. They could do this either in relation to Damian or a made-up situation or character.

- Towards the end of the lesson, bring the class back together to share their sentences.

Differentiation

Support: Give children different, easier words from the book or generally.
Extension: Challenge children to see who can find each word the quickest, before carrying on to do the definition activity.

2. Identifying themes

Objective

To identify a book's themes.

What you need

Copies of *Millions*, photocopiable page 30 'Identifying themes'.

Cross-curricular link

PSHE

What to do

- Start the lesson by asking the children what a 'theme' is in a book (answers could include that it's the message or meaning of a book).

- Explain to the children that books usually have more than one theme. For example, in 'Little Red Riding Hood', one theme could be not to disobey your parents or bad things will happen. Another might be not to talk to strangers. A theme, therefore, could be seen as a message or moral that the author wants you to think about.

- Now give each pair of children a copy of photocopiable page 30 'Identifying themes'. Ask the pairs to brainstorm the themes they think are in *Millions*. They should write one in each of the circles provided (there are four on the sheet but if children can think of more, they can add to these).

- Bring the class back together and sketch out the circles from the sheet on the board. Write the children's suggested themes in the circles. Suggestions might include: grief/sadness; greed/money; family relationships; right versus wrong.

- Next, ask the children to think about what the author is trying to say for each one. Tell them to work in pairs again, writing notes next to or under each circle.

Differentiation

Extension: Ask children if they can think of any other books that share similar themes to those identified in *Millions*.

3. Setting the scene

Objective

To identify and summarise main ideas.

What you need

Media resource 'Setting the scene'.

What to do

- Display the media resource 'Setting the scene' and read the text (taken from Chapter 15) aloud to the children.

- Ask: *What words are repeated in the passage?* ('empty' and there is also 'emptiest') Circle these and ask why the author chose to do this. (to emphasise how empty the place is in Damian's eyes)

- Next, tell the children that, for such a short passage of text, Damian uses a lot of figurative language, especially similes. Ask the class to give you some examples. Possible answers include: 'It was like waking up in the morning a bit late…'; 'That's what it was like, space'; 'It sounded like a submarine'; 'It sounded like a giant drumming on the side of a submarine'.

- Explain that by using all these similes Damian is trying to describe how he feels in the place and to convey how different and foreign it is now – perhaps before coming back he thought it would feel like home but the reality is that it is very different now. Ask: *How does Damian feel to be back in his old house. Is he happy? Sad? Scared? How does his description of the setting reflect his emotions?*

- Invite the children to share their opinions, ensuring they use examples to explain their thoughts.

Differentiation

Extension: Challenge children to either write their own version of this episode or write about a time when they experienced a shocking situation.

4. In the news

Objective

To identify how language, structure and presentation contribute to meaning.

What you need

Copies of *Millions*, media resource 'In the news', photocopiable page 31 'Read all about it!'.

What to do

- Ask the children to read the web article in Chapter 12 of *Millions* where Damian discovers where the money came from.

- Split the class into small groups and display the media resource 'In the news'. Ask the groups to discuss the questions on the screen. When they have done this, call the class back together to share their opinions. Possible answers to the questions are:
  - Because we need to hear an unbiased account of what happened – it allows the reader to see a version of events not filtered by Damian.
  - Answers here will depend on what the children think. It's slightly unusual for a web-based news article to be so long and have so much detail.
  - Sometimes the links to adverts and other news stories come at an important point – a cliffhanger – so it keeps the reader in suspense. The author might have chosen to include them in order to make the article seem more realistic. Some of the links are humorous so perhaps he was trying to make the reader laugh.

- Working independently, ask the children to complete photocopiable page 31 'Read all about it!'. Encourage them to make the article as interesting and dramatic as possible, and invite them to share their articles afterwards.

Differentiation

Support: Let children discuss what they would put in their article instead of writing about it.

5. Dear diary

Objective

To draw inferences about a character's feelings, thoughts and motives.

What you need

Copies of *Millions*, media resource 'What is Dorothy like?', printable page 'Dear diary'.

Cross-curricular link

PSHE

What to do

- Explain to the class that they are going to consider what happens in *Millions* from Dorothy's point of view.

- Ask the children for their thoughts on what Dorothy is like as a person, from the way that Damian has described her in the book. Encourage them to use examples to justify their opinions from events that are written about. For example, perhaps Dorothy could be seen as kind as she realises when Damian is upset in the department store. Maybe she's a good cook because she can make lasagne (even if Anthony doesn't like it!). She makes Damian's dad laugh for the first time in a long time, so perhaps she is a funny person. Write their thoughts and suggestions on the whiteboard.

- Next, open the media resource 'What is Dorothy like?' and read through the text with the class.

- Provide each child with a copy of printable page 'Dear diary'. Ask them to write a diary entry, written by Dorothy, about her recent time spent with the family. Have the media resource open on the interactive whiteboard so that they can refer to it as they complete the sheet.

- Finally, invite volunteers to read out their diary entry to the rest of the class.

Differentiation

Support: Let children write a few short sentences describing Dorothy, based on their opinions of her from the book.

6. What really happened?

Objective

To use spoken language to develop understanding through speculating, hypothesising, imagining and exploring ideas.

What you need

Copies of *Millions*.

What to do

- With the class, re-read the section in Chapter 17 starting 'Dorothy walked past me and into the carriage' (when Damian sees Dorothy getting on a train) to the sentence 'I stepped back and I was still in the living room, where no one was talking' – which is just before Dorothy returns to the house.

- Ask the children to talk in pairs or small groups about what happened during this scene. Did Dorothy really see Damian and change her mind? Did she suddenly feel guilty and return by herself?

- If they can, the children should back up their opinions with any evidence from the text. They can also use their own beliefs – for example, is it really possible to make someone see you when you're not there?

- Next, the children could pretend to be Dorothy and the passengers she encounters on the train. What does she say to them and them to her?

- When they have done this, call the class back together and go through their ideas. You could organise a vote at the end of the lesson to see what the most popular theory is about what happened between Dorothy and Damian at the train station.

Differentiation

Extension: Invite children to pretend to be Dorothy and perform a soliloquy to the class, talking about her strange experience.

7. Author interview

Objective

To ask questions to improve understanding of a text; to participate in role play.

What you need

Copies of *Millions*, media resource 'Author interview'.

What to do

- Tell the class that, today, they are going to think about how to interview an author.

- Explain that you would like them to think about the sort of questions they would ask Frank Cottrell Boyce if they were given the chance to interview him about *Millions*. Point out that the questions should show an understanding of the book – no interviewer wants to get things wrong!

- To get the children started, display the media resource 'Author interview', which sets out some ideas regarding the type of questions that might be asked.

- After the children have jotted down their ideas and questions, invite pairs to have a go at role-playing the situation. One child could take on the role of Frank Cottrell Boyce (and guess his answers based on their own opinions) and the other could act as an interviewer (either themselves or someone else).

- It would be fun and interesting to share some of the role plays with the rest of the class at the end of the lesson.

8. In the news

Objective

To prepare texts to read aloud and to perform.

What you need

Copies of *Millions*.

Cross-curricular link

PSHE, drama

What to do

- With the class, read aloud the section at the beginning of Chapter 13, from when Dorothy (or the bin) says 'Hello, Damian' up to and including when Damian's dad says 'You don't cook. You warm. And if you feel so strongly about it, you can help clear up while the lasagne is cooking.'

- Next, split the class into groups of four and tell them you want them each to take on a role of Damian, Anthony, their dad or Dorothy.

- Ask them to act out their lines from the passage you just read. (They will need to have their books open on the appropriate pages for this.) They don't need to read out the text in between, just the dialogue.

- Encourage the children to pay close attention to how their character may be feeling and convey this through how they speak and their expressions. They can add actions too to their performance – for example, a chopping motion when preparing the lasagne.

- It would be interesting to have the groups perform their dialogues in front of the rest of the class, to see how different individuals portray different characters.

- You could also develop this activity by asking the children to swap roles later on and try being a different character.

Differentiation

Extension: Invite children to make up their own dialogue based on what they've read.

Word detectives

● Next to each word, write down its meaning. On the next line, use the word in a proper sentence.

1. **Saint:**_____

_____

_____

2. **Martyr:** _____

_____

_____

3. **Levitate:**_____

_____

_____

4. **Persecution:** _____

_____

_____

5. **Hermitage:**_____

_____

_____

6. **Enlightening:** _____

_____

_____

Identifying themes

● What are the main themes in *Millions*? Write one theme in each of the circles.

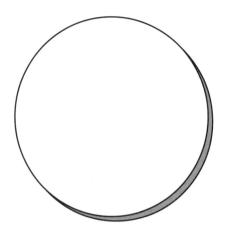

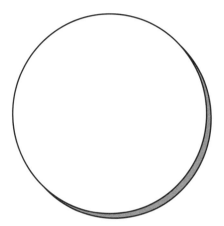

Millions

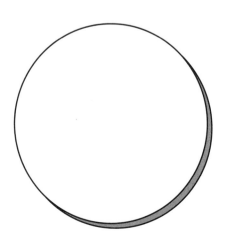

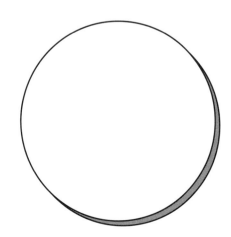

Read all about it!

- Write a few paragraphs in the style of a newspaper, based on the information you read about the robbery. Try to make it as exciting and dramatic as possible and write a catchy title. Don't forget to draw a picture in the box provided.

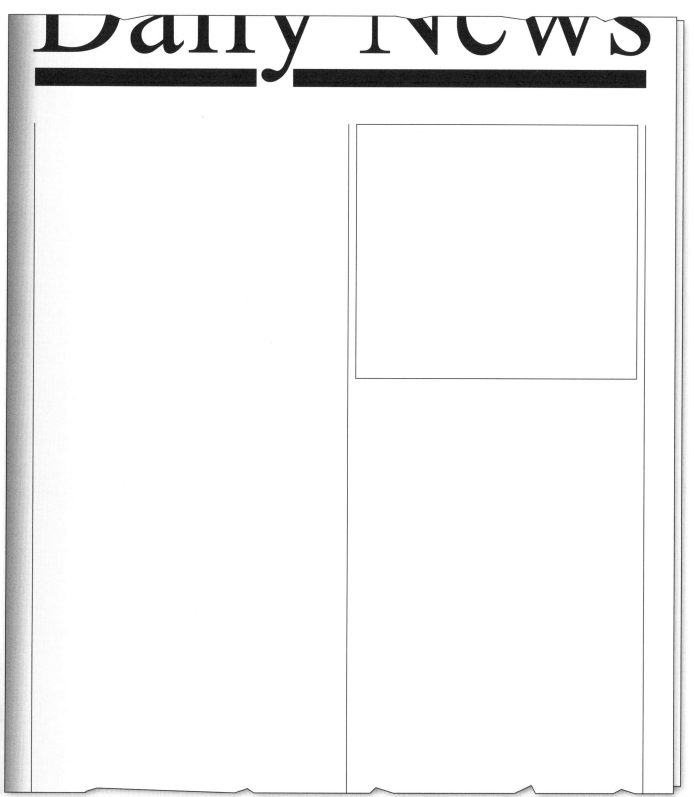

▼ TALK ABOUT IT

1. A different viewpoint

To explore ideas based on a different point of view.

What you need

Copies of *Millions*, media resource 'A different viewpoint', photocopiable page 35 'Anthony's viewpoint'.

Cross-curricular link

PSHE

What to do

- Explain to the children that in this activity they will practise using their oral storytelling skills.

- Ask: *How different do you think the story of* Millions *would be if it were told by Anthony instead of Damian?* Possible answers could include that Anthony (a) would have focused more on the money and what he could buy with it; (b) was worried about Damian's obsession with saints; (c) was angry with Damian for giving the money away; (d) would have talked more about the value of houses and properties.

- Display media resource 'A different viewpoint'. Discuss the five quotations from the book, where Damian explains how the story might be different if Anthony were telling it. Ask: *What can you tell about Anthony from these?* (He focuses on money all the time and likes financial security.) *Why do you think he is like that?* (Some people are just attracted to money more; perhaps he feels insecure following his mother's death.)

- Ask the children to think about how they would tell the story from Anthony's point of view. Invite them to use photocopiable page 35 'Anthony's viewpoint' to prepare a short presentation, summarising the main points and how Anthony would respond to the events.

Differentiation

Support: Let children concentrate on the last chapter only, summarising how they feel about having no more money left.

2. Buying friendship

Objective

To participate in role play.

What you need

Copies of *Millions*.

Cross-curricular link

PSHE, maths

What to do

- Explain to the class that in this lesson they are going to explore how money can influence friendships. Talk about the ways in which Damian and Anthony use money at their new school – by buying people crisps and drinks, asking people to do favours in return for money, and so on.

- Next, ask the children why Damian and Anthony use money like this (perhaps to gain respect and attention in their new school). *Do you think this is a good way to get friends and become known? Why/why not?*

- Ask: *What effect does Damian's and Anthony's spending have on the school?* (Everyone starts asking for money for small favours, and bargaining about the costs. When everyone has money, the money they offer now seems less important.) *What does this tell you about money and spending?* (Money loses its value when more people have it.)

- Organise the class into groups of four or five. In each group, one child should be Anthony or Damian, and the others can play themselves (or a made-up character). Each should say what their prized possession is, and Damian/Anthony should offer money for it. The children can choose whether to accept or refuse the offer. If they accept, they can specify the price they want Damian/Anthony to pay. If they refuse, they should explain why.

- Finally, invite each group to role play the situation in front of the class.

3. Making the right choice

Objective

To articulate and justify answers, arguments and opinions.

What you need

Copies of *Millions,* media resource 'Making the right choice'.

Cross-curricular links

PSHE

What to do

- Explain to the class that there is a lot of talk in *Millions* about being 'good' and 'excellent'. Damian and his father seem to be especially concerned with this. However, at the beginning of Chapter 4, Damian says 'It's not as easy to be good as you might think.' Ask the children why they think this is so.

- Open the media resource 'Making the right choice'. Explain to the children that you would like them to work in small groups to talk about the three different dilemmas on the three separate screens. Read these aloud, then leave them on the screen so the children can discuss their thoughts. (You may need to explain what a moral dilemma is – a problem with different solutions that might be right or wrong based on a person's beliefs.)

- A little later, ask a spokesperson for each group to share their group's thoughts on each of the dilemmas. Invite others in the class to contribute their own views in support or against these. Ensure that everyone remains respectful of each other's opinions.

- Finally, ask the children to share any examples of times when they had to make difficult decisions, based on right or wrong. This could include telling on a friend, owning up to an accident and so on.

4. My chosen saint

Objective

To participate in presentations.

What you need

Copies of *Millions,* photocopiable page 36 'My chosen saint', internet access.

Cross-curricular link

RE, computing

What to do

- Start the lesson by talking about Damian's obsession with saints. Ask: *Why does Damian like to learn about them?* (He is desperate to know if his mother has been made into one.) *Do you know of any saints yourselves?*

- Ask: *Do you think that knowing about saints is interesting – or boring? Does the way Damian talk about the saints in the book make the information more interesting? Why/why not?*

- Invite the children to choose a saint that they find interesting (either from *Millions* or they can use the internet to look for ideas). They should research their saint on the internet, using photocopiable page 36 'My chosen saint' to jot down a few details and interesting facts about them. (Tell them that they do not need to draw a picture of their saint at this point.)

- When they have finished, invite the class to choose their favourite saint. Ask for volunteers to come up to the front to present their saint. Using persuasive language and an enthusiastic tone, they should try to persuade the rest of the class to vote for their saint. You could have various categories, such as 'most impressive miracle', 'best name', and so on.

- For a homework activity, ask the children to draw a picture of their saint in the box provided and write a full paragraph about them, drawing on the notes they made on the sheet.

5. Imaginary friends

Objective

To develop understanding through imagining and exploring ideas.

What you need

Copies of *Millions*, photocopiable page 37 'My imaginary friend'.

Cross-curricular link

PSHE

What to do

- Start the lesson by asking the children: *Do you think Damian really saw the saints he mentioned or did he imagine them?* (There is no right answer to this – it's vague in the book.) Invite them to back up their opinions by referring to points in the text.

- Next, ask the children to work in pairs, discussing if they have ever had an imaginary friend (this might be an animal, person or other being) and to say what their name was, what they were like and what they would do with them. (Note: some children may be reluctant to admit this – if this is the case they can make up an imaginary friend in class instead.)

- Next, hand out photocopiable page 37 'My imaginary friend'. Ask the children to write a short description about their imaginary friend, and draw a picture of them in the box provided.

- Call the class back together and see if anyone is brave enough to talk about their imaginary friend and show the others a picture!

Differentiation

Extension: Challenge children to have a conversation between their imaginary friends in pairs.

6. Knowing what to say

Objective

To participate in role play.

What you need

Copies of *Millions*.

Cross-curricular link

Drama, PSHE

What to do

- With the class, re-read the section in Chapter 17 where Damian visits the department store in which his mother worked, finishing at the sentence 'Which was worse.'

- Tell the class that you would like them to pretend that Damian and the Chanel woman actually did have a conversation, and to re-enact the scenario.

- Organise the children to work in pairs (or, if you like, threes, so Dorothy can also get involved). Before they begin, brainstorm the kind of things Damian and the Chanel woman might talk about. For example, she might:
  - ask Damian how he is
  - say that she's sorry about what happened to his mother
  - ask who Dorothy is.

  Damian could reply by:
  - saying he's OK and ask how she is
  - asking some questions about his mum
  - explaining that Dorothy is a friend.

- Once the children have had a chance to practise what they're going to say, call the class back together again and invite some volunteers to demonstrate their role play in front of the others.

Anthony's viewpoint

● Imagine you are Anthony and it is your turn to tell the story of *Millions*. Prepare a short talk based on your feelings about the following key events.

1. Your mother's death and why you use it to get things.

   _____

   _____

2. Damian's discovery of the money.

   _____

   _____

3. Using the money at school in front of friends.

   _____

   _____

4. What you want to spend the money on.

   _____

   _____

5. What you think of Damian's desire to spend it on charities.

   _____

   _____

6. How you feel when the criminals know about the money.

   _____

   _____

7. How you feel at the end when Damian decides to give the money away.

   _____

   _____

My chosen saint

● Choose your favourite saint from *Millions* (or look for your own), then write a few key points about them in the spaces below. Try to find the most interesting facts possible!

Name: _____

Patron saint of: _____

Dates: _____
(Birth to death)

Country: _____

Biography: _____

_____

_____

_____

_____

Miracles: _____

_____

_____

_____

_____

Why I've picked him/her: _____

_____

_____

_____

My imaginary friend

● Create your own imaginary friend. Write key facts about them and draw a picture.

Name: _____

Age: _____

Likes: _____

_____

_____

Dislikes: _____

_____

Why they are my friend: _____

_____

_____

_____

_____

_____

_____

GET WRITING

1. For sale!

Objective

To plan their own writing.

What you need

Copies of *Millions*, interactive activity 'Estate agent jargon', photocopiable page 41 'For sale!', media resource 'House selling prompts'.

What to do

- Explain that in today's lesson the children are going to attempt a different type of writing.

- Start off by reading aloud the 'Moving house' piece by Anthony at the beginning of Chapter 3 in the book.

- Explain to the children that Anthony uses language like an estate agent in this piece. Ask them if they can find any examples of this. (Answers could include: 'retain its value well', 'cost-efficient', 'substantial', 'exclusive'.) You may need to explain what the words mean if children are unsure.

- What do the children think of this style of language? Is it effective? Interesting? Funny? Encourage them to give and justify their opinions.

- Next, display the interactive activity 'Estate agent jargon'. Invite volunteers to come to the whiteboard to try to match up the estate agent 'speak' with normal adjectives and descriptions.

- Next, hand out copies of photocopiable page 41 'For sale!'. Before completing the sheet, ask the children to brainstorm a description of their own house using the sort of language Anthony or estate agents use. Encourage them to use as many impressive adjectives as possible to try to sell their house!

- Display media resource 'House selling prompts' to help the children as they write their descriptions.

Differentiation

Extension: Challenge children to research houses for sale on the internet and write a more detailed description for homework.

2. Book review

Objective

To assess effectiveness of own and others' writing.

What you need

Copies of *Millions*, book review from a newspaper or magazine, photocopiable page 42 'Book review'.

Cross-curricular link

Art

What to do

- As a class, ask the children what they thought of the book. For example: *What was the book about? What did you like about the book? What did you not like about it? Would you recommend the book to other people? What age range is the book suitable for? How many stars would you rate it, out of five?* Encourage them to be honest – if they did not like the book, it is fine to say so!

- Show the children a book review from a newspaper or online book magazine – one written about children's books should be suitable.

- Ask the children to talk in pairs about what details a good book review should contain, making notes if desired. They should then share these with the rest of the class.

- Write their ideas on the whiteboard and add any of the above questions if appropriate.

- Now distribute photocopiable page 42 'Book review' to the class. Explain that the children should use this sheet to write their own book review of *Millions*, using the knowledge they have gained. (This could also be given as a homework activity if time is short.) Encourage them to draw a picture based on an event from the book in the space provided.

3. If I had £1 million...

Objective

To create settings, characters and plot.

What you need

Photocopiable page 43 'If I had £1 million...', media resource 'Story writing prompts'.

Cross-curricular link

PSHE

What to do

- Explain to the children that people often have various different ideas about how they would spend £1 million. Some people would spend it all, some would save it, some would give it to charity or they might do a mixture of the three. Ask the children what they would do if they had one million pounds. What would they spend it on? Who would they give it to? Why would they save it?

- Next, hand out photocopiable page 43 'If I had £1 million...'. Tell the children that you would like them to plan their own story on a character who had just found £1 million.

- Before they begin, they should think about the structure of a typical story and the sort of person their main character is. Display the media resource 'Story writing prompts' and go through the points with the children. Leave this screen open so that they can refer to it while they write their story outlines on the sheet. They can also sketch images in the boxes if this helps.

- Encourage the children to be as imaginative as possible when creating their characters and story outlines. The main character doesn't even need to be a human if they would rather have an animal or a made-up being (such as an alien or monster).

4. Alternative ending

Objective

To discuss and record ideas.

What you need

Copies of *Millions*, media resource 'Other possible endings', individual whiteboards and pens, printable page 'Alternative ending'.

What to do

- Read the final chapter of *Millions* again with the class, particularly concentrating on what Damian spent the money on: '...with 20,345 new euros we built 14 hand-dug wells in northern Nigeria.'

- Ask the children:
  - Was Dad right to allow Damian to choose what to do with the remaining money?
  - Did Damian spend the money wisely?
  - Do you feel sorry for Anthony?

- Now tell the class that you would like them to imagine a different ending. Working in pairs, they should consider the questions on the media resource 'Other possible endings', discussing their opinions and making notes on their individual whiteboards.

- Finally, ask the children to use their notes to compose their own ending to the story of *Millions*. They can use printable page 'Alternative ending' for this purpose. Ask them to write four paragraphs, as in the original book (Chapter 20). If they would prefer, they can take the action in their ending back to Chapter 19, considering the possibility that Damian *did* keep some money aside. If so, why did he do it?

Differentiation

Support: Let children write some bullet points of the main action, rather than complete paragraphs.

5. Meeting Mum

Objective

To organise paragraphs around a theme.

What you need

Copies of *Millions*, media resource 'Meeting Mum'.

Cross-curricular link

PSHE

What to do

- With the class, re-read the section in Chapter 19 where Damian speaks to his mother.

- Next, display the media resource 'Meeting Mum'. Go through the questions on the first screen with the children, encouraging them to share their ideas and opinions.

- Now tell the children that they are going to write a diary entry from Damian about the meeting with his mother. Encourage them not to merely repeat the information they have read in the book and discussed in class. Instead, they should try to use their senses to place themselves in the scene, as if they were there. As an aid to their writing, let them refer to the prompts provided on the second screen of 'Meeting Mum'.

- Remind the children that using similes and metaphors is a great way of enriching their creative writing. Revise with them what each term means:
  - **Simile:** this is used when you want to say one thing is like something else – such as 'His smile was like the sunshine'.
  - **Metaphor:** this is stronger than a simile because it says one thing *is* another thing, not *like* it – 'He was her sunshine'.

Differentiation

Support: Let children write about the emotions they think they would feel if they were Damian, rather than a continuous piece of prose.
Extension: Challenge children to write a short piece of dialogue between Damian and his mother, with appropriate punctuation.

6. Be persuasive!

Objective

To use simple organisational devices in non-narrative writing.

What you need

Copies of *Millions*, printable page 'Clean and safe', media resource 'Be persuasive!', A4 paper.

Cross-curricular links

Geography, science

What to do

- Ask the children if they can remember what kind of charities Damian donated his money to in the book. (Ones that specialised in providing clean water and digging wells for people in developing countries.) Do they think that this is a good cause? Would they choose this themselves or would they pick another charity? Ask them to explain their reasons.

- With the class, read the information on printable page 'Clean and safe'. Explain any words that are not clear.

- Now tell the class that a person with a lot of money wants to give it to a deserving charity. Give each child a sheet of A4 paper and ask them to write a proposal on it to convince them to donate it to a water-aid organisation (they can make up the name).

- Open the media resource 'Be persuasive!' and together read through the points that the children should include in their proposal. Write the following words as prompts on the whiteboard: Title; Introductory sentence; Subheadings; Conclusion.

Differentiation

Support: Let children simply list some of the benefits of water-aid charities under headings such as: What are wells? Why are they needed? Where are they needed? How do they help people?
Extension: Invite children to research a charity of their choice and apply the same structure in their write-up.

For sale!

● Write an advert for either your own house or a made-up one. Remember to use impressive language to persuade others to buy it! Draw a picture of the house in the box provided.

Book review

- Write a book review for *Millions*.

Title of book: _____

Author: _____

Reviewed by: _____

Who would enjoy this book?

What is the book about?

How many stars would you give this book?

☆ ☆ ☆ ☆ ☆

Draw a picture based on the book.

Did you like the book? Why or why not?

If I had £1 million…

- Create a character and plan a story about them finding £1 million and what they will do with it. Remember to think carefully about how your story will begin, develop and end, what your characters are like, and where it is set.

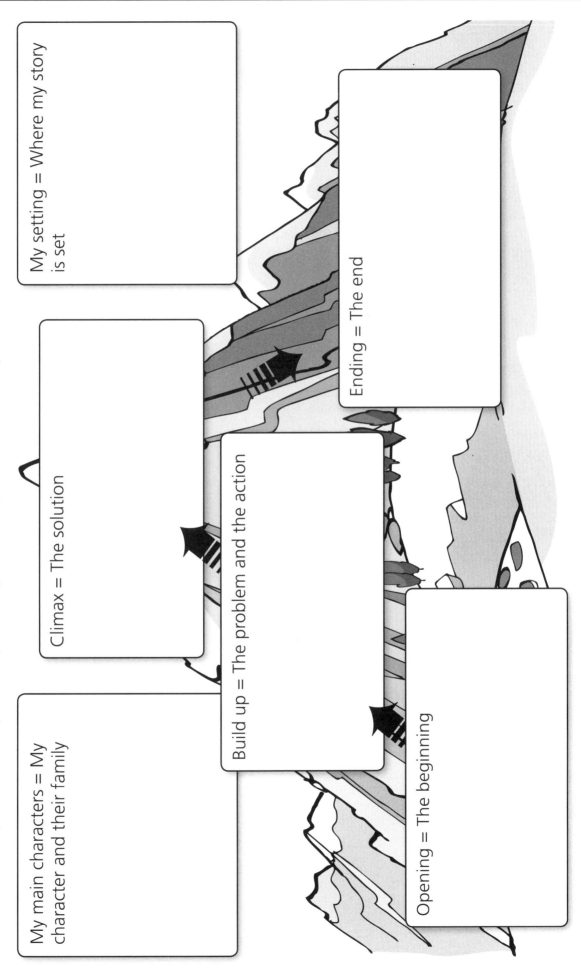

My setting = Where my story is set

Ending = The end

Climax = The solution

Build up = The problem and the action

My main characters = My character and their family

Opening = The beginning

▼ ASSESSMENT

1. Who does it belong to?

To use possessive apostrophes appropriately.

What you need

Printable page 'Who possesses?'.

What to do

- Provide each child with a copy of printable page 'Who possesses'. Tell the children that they are going to revise how to use possessive apostrophes.

- Explain that they have to choose and circle the correct possessive form from the three highlighted words in each sentence.

- Say that in some cases more than one answer could be right but, where possible, they should use their knowledge of the book *Millions* to know which word is the best fit.

- At the end, go through each sentence, explaining why each answer is correct. Answers:
  1. Damian's
  2. robbers' (by context, but could accept robber's)
  3. children's
  4. Mormons' (by context but could accept Mormon's)
  5. people's
  6. burglar's or burglars'
  7. women's
  8. neighbours' (by context, but could accept neighbour's)
  9. Anthony's
  10. wells' (by context, but could accept well's)

2. Wonderful wordsearch

Objective

To revise new vocabulary learned as part of a text.

What you need

Printable page 'Wonderful wordsearch', highlighter pens.

Cross-curricular link

RE

What to do

- Provide each child with a copy of printable page 'Wonderful wordsearch'. Explain that they're going to do a wordsearch based on words they learned as part of their studies on *Millions*.

- Tell the children that there are seven words in the grid that they have already encountered in previous activities. Some are to do with saints and religion, and others are from the real estate activity they did (see activity 1 in the 'Get writing' section).

- Also explain that the words will be scattered around the grid – forwards, backwards and diagonally – so they will have to be sharp-eyed! They will not be given the words to look for as the aim of the activity is to identify words that they have come across previously.

- The words that the children need to find in the grid are: saint, martyr, levitate, hermitage, bedroom, exclusive, garden.

Differentiation

Support: Children who find this activity difficult can be given the words to find in the grid.

3. Simile or metaphor?

Objective
To demonstrate an understanding of figurative language.

What you need
Printable page 'Simile or metaphor?'.

What to do

- Provide each child with a copy of printable page 'Simile or metaphor?'. Tell the children that this activity will test their understanding of the difference between metaphors and similes and how they are used in figurative language.

- Explain that the children need to draw a line from each phrase on the sheet to the correct circle to say whether it is a simile or a metaphor.

- The children should do this individually to test their own knowledge of figurative language.

- When the class has had enough time, go through each phrase with them, asking for the answers. For each incorrect answer, explain why the phrase is a simile/metaphor. Answers:
  - Simile: The children roar like a lion; He talks like a parrot; As poor as a church mouse; She swims like a fish; Damian acts like a saint.)
  - Metaphor: He's a big baby; She's green with envy; His Mum's hair was pure gold; The nurses are angels; They are becoming a pain in the neck.

- To end the lesson, ask the children if they can suggest their own similes or metaphors to share with the rest of the class.

4. Prefix mix-up

Objective
To apply their knowledge of correct prefixes.

What you need
Printable page 'Prefix mix-up'.

What to do

- Provide each child with a copy of printable page 'Prefix mix-up'.

- Explain that someone has tried to write some sentences about *Millions* but has mixed up their prefixes very badly.

- Working on their own, the children should write the word – using a correct prefix – in the box on the line next to each sentence so that everything makes sense.

- At the end of the lesson, go through each sentence with the children, confirming the correct prefix in each case. Answers:
  1. misunderstood
  2. superheroes
  3. illegal
  4. anticlockwise
  5. unenlightened
  6. autobiography
  7. impossible
  8. rewrite

5. Homophones

Objective

To use homophones in the correct context.

What you need

Printable page 'Homophones'.

What to do

- Provide each child with a copy of printable page 'Homophones'. Tell the children that they are going to revise what they have learned about homophones.

- Explain that each sentence has two gaps. The children must choose the correct version of the homophones given to go in each gap and write it in the relevant space.

- Ask the children to work on their own, answering to the best of their ability.

- Once they have finished this activity, go through each question with the class, asking for answers. If children answer incorrectly, ask if someone else knows the right answer. Answers:
  1. there/their
  2. hear/here
  3. two/too
  4. see/sea
  5. knight/night
  6. groan/grown
  7. right/write
  8. heel/he'll

6. Can you remember?

Objective

To recall different aspects of the book.

What you need

Photocopiable page 47 'Can you remember?'.

What to do

- Tell the children that it's time to see how much they can remember about the book *Millions*.

- Provide each child with a copy of photocopiable page 47 'Can you remember?'. Explain to them that, in this activity, they have to use their memory to recall certain details about the book and circle whether the statements on the sheet are true or false.

- For false statements, ask them to provide the correct information on the line below.

- In order to truly test their memory skills, they should attempt this activity without referring to the book. (If necessary, they can refer to their copy later.) Answers:

  1. True
  2. False (Latter Day Saints)
  3. False (Naples)
  4. True
  5. True
  6. False (St Joseph)
  7. True
  8. False (Nigeria)

Differentiation

Support: Children who find it hard to remember the details about the book could just complete the True or False part or, alternatively, you could let them look for the answers in the book.

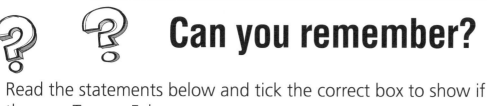

Can you remember?

- Read the statements below and tick the correct box to show if they are True or False.

1. Damian's new school is called Great Ditton Primary. True False

_____

2. The neighbours are members of the Church of Present Day Saints. True False

_____

3. Damian's dad said that pizza was invented in Pisa. True False

_____

4. The shoes that all the children want at school are called Rockports. True False

_____

5. The meal that Dorothy prepares for the family is lasagne. True False

_____

6. Damian plays St Peter in the Nativity Play. True False

_____

7. The policeman always asks for toast when he calls around. True False

_____

8. Damian uses the money to buy wells in Uganda. True False

_____

SCHOLASTIC

Available in this series:

978-1407-16066-5

978-1407-16053-5

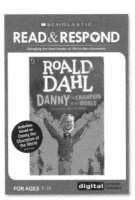
978-1407-16054-2

978-1407-16055-9

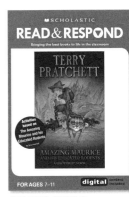
978-1407-16056-6

978-1407-16057-3

978-1407-16058-0

978-1407-16059-7

978-1407-16060-3

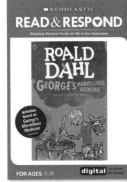
978-1407-16061-0

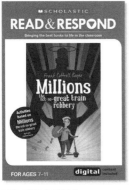
978-1407-16062-7

978-1407-16063-4

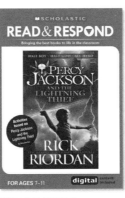
978-1407-16064-1

978-1407-16065-8 **JAN 2017**

978-1407-16052-8 **JAN 201**

978-1407-16067-2 **JAN 2017**

978-1407-16068-9 **JAN 2017**

978-1407-16069-6 **JAN 2017**

978-1407-16070-2 **JAN 2017**

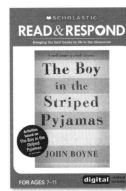

978-1407-16071-9 **JAN 20**

To find out more, call: 0845 6039091
or visit our website www.scholastic.co.uk/readandrespond